Rejoice! Rejoice!

Cathy Lee

Dove Communications

In him
I live
and move
and have
my being

Published by Dove Communications
60-64 Railway Rd., Blackburn, Victoria, 3130

Designed by Keith Lucas
Photographs courtesy of John and Lesley Spradbrow,
Leo Kiriloff, the Catholic Audio-Visual Centre,
Sydney, and the Advocate Press, Melbourne
Illustrations by Elizabeth O'Flynn
Songs used in the book courtesy of Moira Eastman and
Wendy Poussard ('Mary's Song'); Shirley Macdonald and Eva Adams
('The Spirit is coming')
Biblical texts from The Jerusalem Bible, Darton, Longman & Todd, London
Typeset by Bookset, Melbourne
Printed in Australia by Globe Press, Brunswick

National Library of Australia
Cataloguing-in-Publication data

Lee , Cathy.

Rejoice Rejoice

ISBN 0 85924 230 7
1. Public workshop. 2. Religious dance, Modern.
I. Title.

264

Nihil Obstat:	Frank T. O'Loughlin, S.T.D., Diocesan Censor.
Imprimatur:	Peter J. Connors, D.C.L., Vicar General, Archdiocese of Melbourne.
Date:	13th September, 1983.

The *Nihil Obstat* and *Imprimatur* are official declarations
that a book or pamphlet is free of doctrinal or moral error.
No implication is contained therein that those who have
granted the *Nihil Obstat* and *Imprimatur* agree with the
contents, opinions, or statements expressed. They do not
necessarily signify that the work is approved as a basic text
for catechetical instruction.

Foreword

'In the beginning God created the heavens and the earth. Now the earth was a formless void and there was darkness over the deep. God's Spirit hovered over the water.'

Darkness . . . silence . . . stillness. At the beginning stands the great dancer. There is nothing before his dance begins. Then from the very heart of the·dancer flows a song that bursts from his lips, shattering the empty silence of the void and to the sound of his own song the dance begins; the great dance of creation.

The song rises and falls with the mood and the rhythm of the dancer and, as he moves, the darkness that surrounds him is broken and he dances in the light of the first day. As he leaps and turns, the fullness of his life pours out to fill every corner of the void. What was emptiness is now saturated with his life. Every sweep of his hand embraces the heavens, the steps of his feet mould the earth.

The dancer flows across the earth like water, giving life wherever he passes. With every footfall, the earth beneath him explodes into life, filling the void with colour and movement. Creation now joins in the dance and echoes the moods of the dancer.

The song quickens, the dancer becomes more intense and every ounce of his energy is given to the dance. When the mood changes and the dance slows, the great dancer no longer dances alone, others dance with him, mirroring his movements and joining his song.

'God created man in the image of himself,
in the image of God he created him,
male and female he created them.'

Genesis 1:27

The dancer withdraws and leaves his creation to dance on with 'the dancers of the earth' to lead the song. But with the great dancer gone, the 'dancers of the earth' soon forget the steps, and change the song. Each dances their own way and their steps no longer have the beauty of the first dance but are awkward and hollow. The dance ceases to create; it perverts and destroys.

And so the dancer returns and once again dances on the earth:

'The Word was made flesh,
he lived among us,
and we saw his glory,
the glory that is his as the only Son of the Father,
full of grace and truth.'

John 1:14

His second dance is even more beautiful than the first. For it is a dance of re-creation. The dancer moves as if possessed by life. He meant us never to forget his dance again. Everything he touched took up his dance of life.

But the dance offended, the dance defied and on a tree the dancer died.

But death could not stop the dance. The dance possessed the dancer and he danced beyond the cross and we saw his glory and we took up his dance.

Chris Uhlmann

Contents

Introduction

Rejoice, Rejoice! is a beginners handbook for those who are interested in or involved in beginning liturgical movement in their school, classroom or parish.

The dances described are easy to follow and learn, and are so choreographed that anyone can join in.

It is hoped the person using the handbook will take the ideas and change and adapt them to suit his or her own situation.

What is liturgical dance?

I suppose that I could best answer this by saying what liturgical dance is for me.

'In him we live and move and have our being.'

Acts 17:28

In the dance, I move freely with him, released from the tensions and worries of the day; separated from life, I am joined in oneness with my Creator. In this rising and joining my God in the dance, I try to lift the congregation with me so that they too can feel the strength of his touch in their lives.

To me, the dance is a gift from God; one that I share with others. It is an expression that comes from deep within my very being. It is creative prayer. It is my prayer. It is exposing myself and my relationship with my Creator to others.

It is a three-way communication between God, myself and his people.

It is accepting an invitation from God to help others to see him more clearly. It is following the creative Christ: the one who taught using parables and images from everyday life. He prodded the imaginations of those around him and allowed understanding to grow in each of them. In the dance, I challenge others to accept his invitation to walk with him.

In the dance, my partner is silent, invisible. He is the leader of the dance, guiding me through every step and movement. It is in him that I live and move and have my being.

Movement prayers

Quite often in the classroom, we may finish a theme by asking the children to make up their own prayers. These prayers may be displayed on the pinboard or they might surround a large mural on the theme. The prayers may be used in a liturgical setting or perhaps written into the children's own workbooks.

Have you ever thought of asking the children to 'dance' their prayers?

Think of a word; perhaps 'joy'.

What do we think of when we say the word 'joy'?

Can you recall times when you were full of joy?

What kind of facial expressions do we have when we are full of joy?

Can you think of an action or gesture to show the word 'joy'?

It may be a leap into the air, or a twirl on the spot with your arms raised into the air.

See how many different actions or gestures you can find to show the word 'joy'.

Let's take another word. Let's try 'Alleluia'. What action or gesture could you use to show the word 'Alleluia'? How many different ways can you show 'Alleluia'? What does the word mean?

Make a list of words with your class and see if you can find appropriate gestures to express these words. Your list may include words like:

Praise
Father
Love
Forgiveness
Peace

After you have finished exploring as many words and movements as you can, you are now ready to proceed further.

If you were to go to your Bible and turn to the book of Psalms, you would find many beautiful quotations that invite you to lift your hands to praise God using your voices and your whole body.

Browse through the psalms and choose a line that specially appeals to you, e.g. psalm 47:

'Clap your hands, all you peoples,
acclaim God with shouts of joy'

or Psalm 106:

'Give thank to Yahweh, for he is good,
his love is everlasting'

Ask the class to think of suitable gestures to bring these two quotations alive with movement. You may be able to compose some psalms of your own and choreograph movement to them.

Remember:

It is not important that the children have a gesture and action for every word.

It is important for the children and teacher to realise that these movement prayers must come from within themselves.

It is a good idea to keep the phrases short and simple.

Movement prayers can be done individually or in groups. They could occasionally take the place of formal classroom prayers. They are an ideal way to conclude a theme and can also be used during Mass for the responsorial psalm. (This, of course, depends on the ruling of your bishop.)

Groups of children I have worked with have written their own 'litany of thanks' and choreographed simple gestures to accompany it:

Thank you, God, for flowers that grow,
     for stars that shine,
     for birds that sing,
     for the gift of life.

Here is a movement prayer for you to try:

Psalm 86

Hear, O Lord, and answer me,

For I am poor and needy;

Guard my life for I am devoted to you,

You are my God, I your servant who trusts in you.

13

Moving to Psalms

More than ever if one hears of a liturgical dance taking place, it has been danced to a hymn — words and music. Liturgical dance can be more than just that. It is now time that we explored other possibilities for movement.

In this chapter, we will look at a psalm and how movement can enhance and bring to life the Word of God.

There are many possibilities here. One way is for the psalm to be read by the leader. When the reader reaches the response (assuming that it is a responsorial psalm), all could join in simple arm gestures which have been choreographed and taught beforehand. These gestures would in some way fit the words of the response.

Another possibility is for the reader to read the psalm while a group or even one dancer interprets it through bodily gestures. For this to be done well, it is necessary for the dancers and the reader to rehearse together so that the reader will be reading at a pace that suits the dancers as well as observing the necessary pauses.

A third possibility is that the dancer may wish to learn the psalm and recite it himself/herself as it is being interpreted. This takes a great deal of skill and is not easy to do.

Here is a simple movement that has been choreographed to Psalm 8. The text is from the *Jerusalem Bible*.

Reader	Dancer
Yahweh, Our Lord,	Dancer stands still, facing the front. Arms are lifted up high into the open 'V' position. Feet together.
how great your name throughout the earth!	Moving the feet apart swing both arms down to side and back up the 'V' position crossing them in front of your chest as you do so.
Above the heavens is your majesty chanted	Bring both arms vertically above your head.
by mouths of children,	Feet together again. Bring hands into lips with palms facing outwards.
babes in arms.	Bring arms down to stretch diagonally towards the ground.
You set your stronghold firm against your foes to subdue your enemies.	Feet apart again and bring your arms up over your head clenching your fist and one hand holding the other wrist.
I look at the heavens made by your fingers,	With feet still apart lunge to the right keeping the right hand down to the side. Take the left arm across the body and up high and down to the left side.
at the moon and stars you set in place.	Repeat the above movement to the left.
Ah, what is man that you should spare a thought for him,	Standing up straight with feet together, bow head and bring arms back to stretch diagonally down to the ground.
the son of man that you should care for him?	Stretch arms forward.
You made him little less than a god,	Kneel on left knee and bow over body slightly with hands into the centre of chest.
You have crowned him with glory and splendour,	Continue to kneel but raise arms to the upward 'V' position.
made him Lord over the work of your hands,	Stand and, with feet together, keep left arm to side and take right arm across body and extend it forward back to the right side.
set all things under his feet.	Bring hands back diagonally stretching down to the ground.

This is only a simple idea as to what can be done with psalms. I encourage you to explore other psalms and finds ways in which you can add gestures and movement.

Even though there is room for spontaneous movement, if the psalm is to be used in a liturgical setting, then as I mentioned before, rehearsing is most important. Timing is crucial. The pauses between each thought and movement have to be carefully timed so that the psalm still continues to flow without losing its meaning.

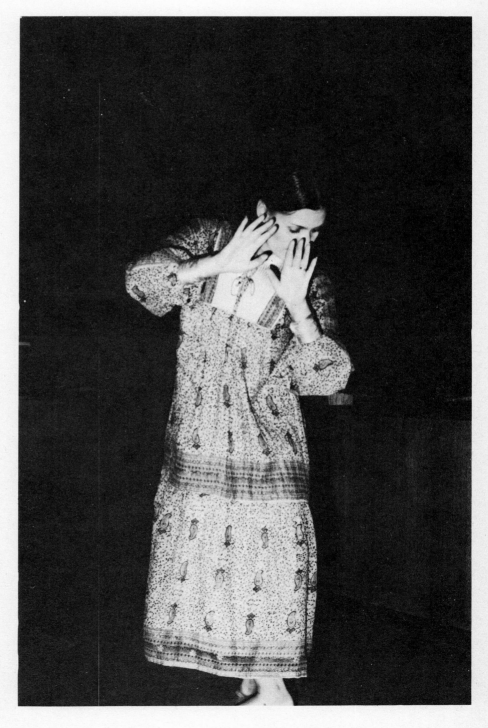

Dance in the Eucharistic Liturgy

The ideas expressed in this chapter are from various liturgies where I have been involved in planning, either with children or with adults. I must point out, however, that the implementation of these ideas depends on the ruling of your local bishop.

> 'To promote active participation, the people should be encouraged to take part by means of acclamations, responses, psalms, antiphons, hymns, as well as by actions, gestures and bodily attitudes; and at proper times a reverent silence should be observed.'
>
> *Vatican 11: Document on Sacred Liturgy*, Para 30.

For dance in the Eucharistic Liturgy to be truly successful, it must be incorporated into the Mass in such a way that it adds to the flow of the liturgical action and does not detract from it.

The dance should be a beautiful and moving experience to those watching.

Dance is a visual expression and it is important that it should be done well. If it isn't, the congregation will find it hard to understand the message that you are trying to convey in your dance. They will find it difficult to pray as they watch you, and you will not have been successful in leading them in prayer.

As a minister of church music should always pray the music before playing it, it is just as important that the dancer should pray the dance before dancing it.

Gestures

Some of the gestures that we use in our dances can be best described through the following pictures.

(Note that these are only *examples*. Do not limit yourself to one or two gestures for concepts as enormous as God. There is no limit to the vocabulary of the body.

Father

Here, the children are making their whole body into a funnel, opening themselves up to God their Father so that his love can pour out through them.

sus
Two gestures are used here: aking the whole body into a cross making a cross using only your nds.

oly Spirit
The Holy Spirit can be shown by o gestures also: the dove, made the hands crossing, and the ague of fire.

Working with children and adults over the past two years, I have used the following simple plan to choreograph dances.

1. We look at the hymn we have chosen to dance to and we read the words over and over, reflecting upon the words as we read them. We ask ourselves: What is the hymn saying? What is the message it is trying to convey?
2. If the hymn is scripturally based, we go to our Bibles and read the whole chapter so that we get a clearer picture of the message in the hymn.
3. We come together as a group to pray.
4. We work together as a group to choreograph the dance steps.

Each time we rehearse the dance, it is a prayer. We can only dance a prayer if we have first prayed through our dance.

The most important times for singing in the Eucharistic Liturgy are at the *acclamations*. Singing helps the whole community to express itself at the high points of the celebration. Singing the *acclamations* highlights and intensifies our worship experience.

The *acclamations* are:

1. The verse before the Gospel
2. The 'Holy Holy'
3. The Memorial Acclamation
4. The Great Amen.

Here are a few ideas that you may find useful in planning movement in your liturgies. Keep in mind that you would not attempt to do all of these in one liturgy.

The Gospel Acclamation

In the Liturgy of the Word, the main event is the proclaiming of the Gospel. Here Christ himself is present and speaks to each one of us as we hear his Word proclaimed in the reading.

To greet the Good News, we stand and sing the Alleluia verse. There are several ways in which the verse before the Gospel can be highlighted and intensified. Here are two suggestions for a Gospel procession:

1. Recently in one Sunday Parish Liturgy, we used the hymn 'Sing Alleuia to the Lord'. This song can be found on the *Praise* album by Maranatha Records. Two dancers were placed halfway down the aisle with the acolyte standing behind them, holding the Gospel book up high. Two more dancers were placed in the right hand aisle of the church and another two on the left hand side. As the music commenced, all the dancers followed by the acolyte began to process slowly up the aisle in time to the music. As the acolyte reached the sanctuary, he continued to walk up the steps and stood further apart from the dancers. The dancers continued to dance on the sanctuary occasionally directing their movements towards the acolyte with the book. At the end of the dance, the acolyte moved forward and joined the dancers in the middle of a circle. The book was raised up high for all to see. The dancers then gathered around the book and once again directed their movements towards it.

2. Another possibility for movement in the Gospel procession is one that the whole congregation can do without moving from their seats.

While the actual procession is taking place, the congregation can:

Bow slightly, bringing their hands into their chests, fingers near their hearts.

Then raise their bodies to a straight standing position and bring their hands to their lips.

Finally, take their hands to their foreheads and open up their arms to the open 'V' position.

Here the whole congregation are opening themselves up, through their gestures, to hear the Word of God.

The 'Holy Holy'

The 'Holy Holy' comes at the end of the Preface. It should be sung by the whole congregation including the Celebrant.

There are many fine versions of this Acclamation that would be suitable for gestures. Although dance may also be introduced at this point, I personally prefer gestures for the whole congregation.

When dancing the 'Holy Holy', it is important to note that the dance should commence immediately after the final words of the Preface, 'we join the angels and saints in proclaiming your glory as we sing (and dance) . . .' There must be no delay between the Celebrant's final words and the beginning of the dance. The dancers should be ready to begin before the Preface.

Here are some gestures that once again can be done by the whole congregation while they are singing the 'Holy Holy'. These gestures can be adapted and changed to suit your own particular musical version. They can also be done without music.

Holy, holy, holy Lord,	While standing, bring your arms up into the 'V' position.
God of Power and might,	Bow slightly over and bring your hands down into a prayer position.
heaven and earth are full of your glory.	Swing your arms back up into the 'V' position and at the same time straighten your body.
Hosanna in the highest.	Bring your arms down a little and raise them up high again.
Blessed is he who comes in the name of the Lord.	Fold your arms across your chest and bow slightly.
Hosanna in the highest.	Raise your arms and finish in the 'V' position.

The Memorial Acclamation

'Let us proclaim the mystery of faith.'

Here the whole community proclaim their beliefs about Christ: he died, he rose, and he will come again.

I feel that dancing at this point would interfere too much with the flow of the Eucharistic Prayer. Once again, however, the congregation could participate more fully by doing some gestures to this acclamation. Here are a few ideas:

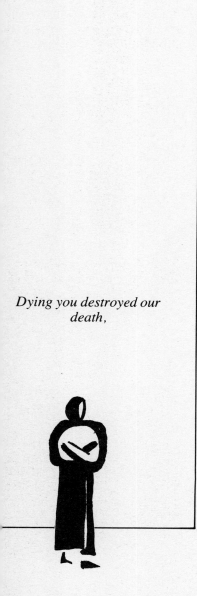

Dying you destroyed our death,

Rising you restored our life.

Lord Jesus, come in glory.

You will find that the gestures outlined in the previous page will also fit the other Memorial Acclamations.

The Great Amen

The congregation could join hands and raise them above their heads as a sign of their unity in faith.

The Introductory Rites

Opportunities for dance in the Introductory Rites are as follows.

The Entrance Hymn

Within the Introductory Rites, the opening hymn and the prayer ar[e] most important parts and therefore should be highlighted.

If the Entrance Hymn is danced, remember that the dance should se[t] theme for the entire Celebration. The dance and the hymn should refle[ct] unity and our coming together.

Often when the Entrance Hymn is sung, there is an unfortunate tend[ency] to finish the hymn as soon as the Celebrant reaches the sanctuary. The h[ymn] and the dance should continue for at least one or two more verses to allo[w] the Celebrant and the ministers to join in the singing of the hymn fro[m] sanctuary.

The Gloria

This is a hymn of praise and is best sung. It is used on Sundays and feasts that do not fall during Lent and Advent. If danced, it should not lengthen the Introductory Rites unduly. When choosing to dance a Gloria, remember to try and choose one that has a repeated antiphon. This allows for greater participation from the congregation at this point. Otherwise, I would choose one that the whole congregation can sing. If dancing the Gloria with a repeated antiphon, why not teach the congregation gestures that they can all join in with as the antiphon comes round? Carey Landry's childrens Gloria from *Bloom Where You Are Planted* is a good example. Sometimes the Gloria can be said while a group of dancers or even one dancer expresses the Gloria through movement. Here is an example of this:

eader	Dancer
lory to God in the highest,	Dancer with both feet together raises both arms high into an open 'V' position.
d peace to his people on earth.	Bring arms down to stretch out forward towards the people.
rd God, heavenly King, mighty God and Father,	With feet still apart, take both arms up to stretch up high over head with hands joined together.
e worship you, we give you anks, we praise you for your ory.	Bring hands into chest and bow over slightly. Straighten body and bring hands to extend forward, turn palms over to face ground and raise hands up high over head.
rd Jesus Christ, only Son of the ather,	Bring hands crossed over chest.
rd God, Lamb of God, you take vay the sins of the world:	Extend arms out to side to form a cross.
ve mercy on us;	Bring hands into centre of chest and bow over.
u are seated at the right hand of e Father:	Extend right hand up diagonally.
ceive our prayer.	Two hands together stretched out forward and raise them up high.
r you alone are the Holy One,	Keeping hands up high, shape them to form a crown.
u alone are the Lord,	Open arms to the 'V' position.
u alone are the Most High, Jesus rist,	Bring arms down and raise up again to the same position quickly.
th the Holy Spirit in the glory of d the Father.	Make a tongue of fire with hands and bring it down slowly.
nen.	Join hands in a prayer position.

The Responsorial Psalm

Many beautiful hymns have been based on the psalms. The psalms provide us with the opportunity to combine mime and dance together. Remember to observe a suitable period of silence between the Old Testament reading and the reading of the psalm.

Once again choose a version of the psalm that has a repeated antiphon that can be sung by all. The congregation could be taught the gestures to be done by them as the antiphon is said. (See movement prayers page 00.)

A second opportunity for movement in the Liturgy of the Word is through the readings and the Gospel. This will be explained in the chapter on Mime.

Our Father, who art in heaven,
(arms up into a 'V' position)

The Communion Rite

In the Communion Rite, there are two opportunities for dance. These are at the Lord's Prayer and also the Thanksgiving Song.

The Lord's Prayer may be sung and danced by a group of people alone; however, I prefer to have the entire congregation recite or sing it while doing the following gestures.

We tried this in one parish. We were aware that the people had not been exposed to movement before so we knew that we had to proceed slowly. Only one gesture was attempted at any one time. Gradually, over a period of a few weeks, the whole congregation had mastered and felt at ease doing the gestures to the Lord's Prayer.

hallowed be thy name;
(keep arms up, palms facing
out, framing God's name)

thy kingdom come; thy will
be done on earth
(bring arms slowly down
in front of you)

as it is heaven.
(raise arms up in front of you)

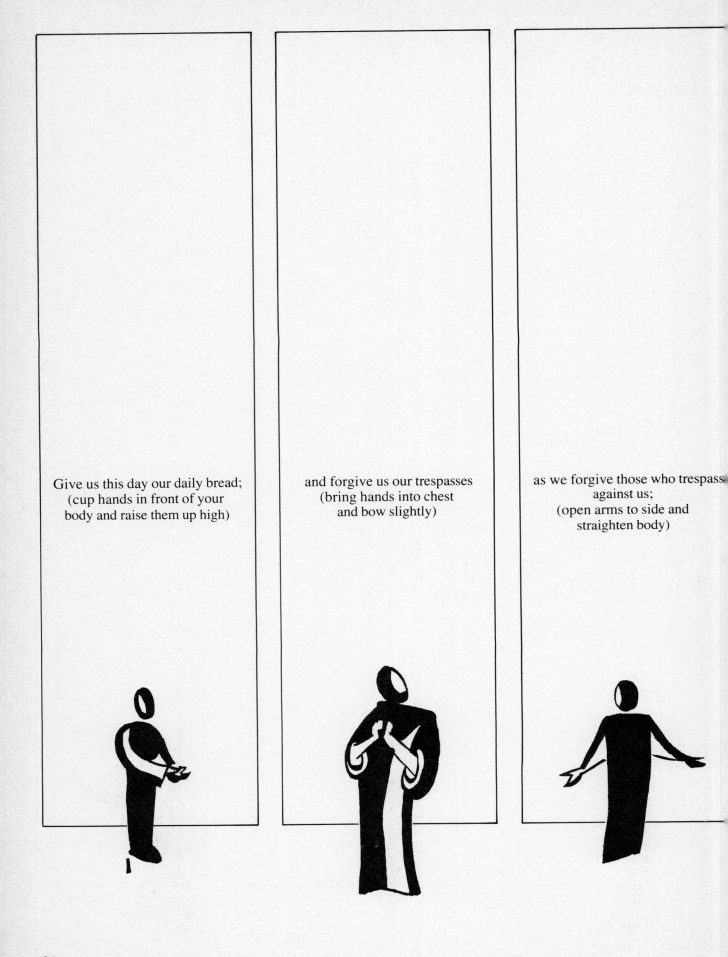

Give us this day our daily bread;
(cup hands in front of your
body and raise them up high)

and forgive us our trespasses
(bring hands into chest
and bow slightly)

as we forgive those who trespass
against us;
(open arms to side and
straighten body)

and lead us not into temptation
(hands across your face)

but deliver us from evil.
(hands raised high)

For yours is the kingdom the
power and the glory,
now and forever.
(swing arms across your body
and raise them up high)

Opinions may vary here, but when dancing the Lord's Prayer in a liturgy, I prefer to use a version that the congregation know and can join in the singing. The above gestures are simple and I have used them with many different musical versions. Timing may have to be changed slightly to fit the music.

Song of Thanksgiving

If there has been a fair amount of singing by the congregation during Communion, then I would suggest that reflective music be played and danced to at this time. A period of silence should surround the Thanksgiving dance. This is of special importance. On the other hand, if music has been played during the distribution of Communion, then a suitable hymn can be chosen to dance to. Alternatively, a prayer, a psalm or a poem can be read or mimed at this point.

On the Feast of the Assumption one year, I was fortunate to see a very moving mime movement done to the poem 'Mary, Joy of all Creation' from the book of the same name published by Dove Communications.

One student read the poem as a flute was played softly in the background. Another student did simple reflective mime movements to express the lines of the poem. Many people were touched by this prayerful presentation.

It is not necessary to sing at this time. Once again, a litany of thanks (mentioned earlier) can be choreographed for this moment.

The Preparation of Gifts

I have left the preparation of gifts until last as the rite is of secondary importance. It should be over and done with as quickly as possible so that it is seen to be only secondary. It is because of this that I do not encourage long dances at this point.

Dancers may be involved in a small and simple procession. Dancing during the procession would only lengthen the rite unnecessarily and would overshadow the primary rites of the Liturgy of the Word and the Liturgy of the Eucharist.

Planning

The most important things to remember when planning dance in the Eucharistic Liturgy are:

> Do not overload the Liturgy with too many dances. It is better to do one dance well than a few dances that are not well prepared and rehearsed.
>
> Always surround your dance with a period of silence. Creating the atmosphere to minister in dance is of vital importance.
>
> Ask yourself: does a dance best express the message I am trying to convey *or* can it best be expressed through a drama, song or mime?

Even though I see the place for solo or group dances, I also feel the need for greater congregational participation in the Liturgy. Here is an example when the whole congregation can join actively, using simple arm gestures:

P. The Lord be with you.
C. And also with you.

P. Lift up your hearts.
C. We lift them up to the Lord.

P. Let us give thanks to the Lord our God.
C. It is right to give him thanks and praise.

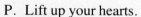

Other times when the whole congregation can join in could be:

Entrance Hymn
Response of the Responsorial Psalm
Antiphon to the Gloria
Lord, have mercy
Verse before the Gospel
Holy, holy, holy
Memorial Acclamation
Great Amen
Our Father.

I think it is important to mention that when beginning to lead congregations in movement, it is best to lead them slowly and gently. Sometimes you may find that they are not ready to use movement. Do not become discouraged at this. In one parish where the dance group minister once a month, it has taken us almost a year to lead the congregation in movement. We started simply with the sign of the cross. This is one dance that we all do but I sometimes wonder if people know the true and powerful meaning behind this sign. We then went on to simple gestures to the Our Father. We started with just simply raising our hands just as the priest does. After a few weeks when people felt comfortable with this movement, we took them on to the next. Some people may never join in; people move at different times.

Remember also not to overload your liturgy with too many gestures from the congregation. After they have learnt a few, you can vary the gestures to add more variety to the liturgy.

Mime

There are many ways in which Jesus speaks to us in the Scriptures. We can read and reflect upon the words, we can sing about the message contained within them or we can mime the stories.

I suppose that in your classroom as teachers or catechists or parish liturgy leaders you have at some time used mime to illustrate a point or as a way of communicating the Gospel message. But, have you really ever taken a deeper look at mime? Have you taken time to see into the silence and gestures unfolding before your eyes?

In a Gospel mime, the mimist interacts within the frame of the Scripture passage. Because the mime is silent, a lot is left to the imagination of the watcher. In our minds, we substitute the words that are missing. We interpret the story as it speaks to us. The mimist helps us to see the Gospel scene. Through his gestures and facial expressions, he touches the hearts and minds of each of us. Through him we hear, see and feel the presence of Jesus in our lives. We watch him give sight to the blind, heal the leper, caress the child and die for the world. Each of us watching the mimist at work interprets his message differently.

Mime focuses our attention to the face and the body; the rest falls away. Each day we are faced with moments when words fail us . . . the beautiful sunset, the newborn child, the love between two people. In our churches we look at the hanging cross and see the silent suffering of Jesus.

Our liturgy already has moments of silence when mime gestures are used: the genuflection, the sign of the cross, the crosses we make before the proclamation of the Gospel, the raising of the book, the sign of peace, the elevation of the gifts, the kissing of the table. To use mime in the liturgy is simply to add to what we already have.

Mime is not dance although they are very closely related, but like dance it cannot be forced upon the congregation. They must be led skilfully and gently. The right environment needs to be created; people need to be drawn into the experience. The mime needs to be well rehearsed and the gestures clear and precise.

Sometimes a 'white face' can be used by the mimist. This needs to be explained to the unsuspecting congregation. The white face immediately wipes away any differences. The mimist is neither male nor female. The white face unites us all.

At Mass, mime could be best used during the Liturgy of the Word, either to proclaim the Gospel or to highlight one of the readings, perhaps even the psalm. Remember too that it can be used as an aid to the homily.

There are many different types of mime. Here are some that we can use in our liturgical celebrations.

Silent Mime

This seems to be the most common type of mime used in Masses and with children in schools. Silent Mime is when we reproduce Scripture without using words. For example, the story of Lazarus who was raised from the dead by Jesus, or the blind man, Bartimaeus. With Silent Mime, we simply take the story as it is. This is a very simple form of mime.

Narrative Mime

Here we combine both narration and mime. The narrator is independent of the mime. Before our eyes, the mimist unfolds the Gospel text as the story is being told. The Easter readings are ideal for this type of mime.

Musical Mime

Appropriate music can be added to a mime. The music, if chosen properly, can help to relate the message of the mime. At an Easter workshop, we mimed the last few days in Jesus' life. We started with the events of Palm Sunday and went through to Good Friday. The whole mime took no longer than three to four minutes. The music I chose was the Gloria from the record *Come To The Quiet* by John Michael Talbot. The piece of music has the distinct sound of a bell ringing in the background. The participants in the mime felt that the bell reminded them of time passing by. People watching the mime felt that through the music and the action taking place before them, they had entered into Jesus' suffering in a very special way.

Spin-off Mime

In a Spin-off Mime, we attempt to bring the Word of God into our lives today. We use people and places familiar to us to unfold the Scriptures. One story that lends itself very well to this type of mime is the parable of the Good Samaritan. Spin-off Mime can be silent or musical.

Here is an example of a mime used in a classroom. The mimist in this case was dressed as a clown, and the mime was of the parable of the sower from Matthew 13:4-9 and 18-23.

The mimist enters and faces the people. By his gestures he invites them to *watch* and *listen*. He then looks around the room and sees a large sack in one corner. He asks the people what is in the bag. He goes over to the bag and drags it back to the centre of the room. The bag is very, very heavy. The mimist shows this by his movements. He opens the bag and looks in, occasionally giving a cheeky grin to the people watching. Slowly, ever so slowly, out of the sack he pulls a heavy sign which reads 'SEEDS'. He shows the sign to the people, holding it up with great difficulty for all to see. He gestures towards the people inviting them to read what is on the sign. Finally he takes the sign and places it to one side. Walking back to the bag, he places one hand well inside it and very slowly produces some imaginary seeds. He then proceeds to scatter the seeds in one small section of imaginary soil. He then begins to water the seeds slowly. Once this is done, he channels the sun's rays down upon the seeds. Finally, dusting himself off he sits down crossed legged in front of the seeds and waits patiently with a smile on his face.

After a few seconds he looks at his wrist (time) and back again at the seeds. He then stands and paces backwards and forwards glancing every now and then at the seeds. By this time, his facial expression should have changed so that people watching are aware that he is growing very impatient. He then faces the people and poses the question: 'Why won't the seeds grow?' He then gets an idea and goes back to the seeds and picks up a few grains of soil and lets it sift through his fingers. His face grows sad. He stands and goes over to the sack. Putting his hand in the sack he produces a sign which reads 'CLAY'. He shows this sign to the people. Then he places the sign on the lifeless seeds.

He then goes back to the sack and brings out some more imaginary seeds. He scatters these seeds in another patch of soil. In the same manner, he waters them and channels the sun's rays to come down upon them. This time he falls asleep. After a few moments, he opens one eye and then another. His expression changes to one of astonishment as he indicates by his movements that the seeds are growing. He kneels in front of his growing seeds looking at them lovingly. Suddenly . . . he indicates that they have fallen over. He tries to make them stand up again but they continue to fall over. Once again he faces the people and asks 'Why?' He goes back to the seeds and picks up a grain of soil and once again lets it sift through his fingers. He shakes his head and reaches into the sack and pulls out another sign which reads 'SANDY'. He places this over the seeds.

This time he plants a third patch of seeds. Once again he goes through the motions of watering them and channelling the sun's rays upon them. He then indicates to the people that more water may be needed. He goes off to the side and fills his bucket with water. On his return he looks at his seeds only to find they have started to grow but are being choked at the bottom by thorns. To show this he indicates his seeds and then places both hands around his own neck in a choking action. A certain amount of overdramatising is needed at this point. Finally he stops and looks at his seeds and weeps. He then pulls from the sack another sign which reads 'THORNS'. He places this on the dead seeds.

Once again he goes back to his sack and brings out the last of the seeds. Again he plants them and waters them. The sun's rays once again come down upon them. He then takes up a sitting position in front of the seeds and waits. After a few seconds, the seeds begin to grow . . . and grow . . . and grow. The mimist indicates this by starting in a crouched position and then growing and growing until finally he indicates that the plants have grown even taller than himself. He stands back and looks proudly at his crop. He goes over to his sack and pulls out and displays another sign which reads 'RICH SOIL'. He then places this on his seeds.

The mimist then goes over to the sack and looks in. He indicates that there is still one thing left inside the sack. What is it? He proceeds to gently lift out a Bible. He holds it high, caresses it near to him and holds it up high again. He then indicates to the people that when they hear the Word of God are they like the 'SANDY SOIL', the 'CLAY SOIL', 'THORNS' or the 'RICH SOIL'? The mimist then gathers his sack and leaves the room.

This mime has worked on several occasions with upper Primary children in the classroom as well as being used as a Gospel mime in a liturgy.

Sometimes when trying to introduce movement into parish liturgies, people are more inclined to accept a mime in preference to a dance. If you are having trouble introducing movement, perhaps the simple mime is the best place to start.

For those of you who would like to experiment with and use the 'white face', here is what you will need:
1. Greasepaint: this is available from most theatrical costume centres or ballet shops. You will need to buy a white base and a jar of black. White pan make-up can also be used but mask will not be as heavy as with greasepaint. Liquid white make-up can also be used. Leichner is a well known brand, and Max Factor for the pan make-up. Some paints can be removed with water, others with remover.
2. Some small brushes.
3. Talcum Powder.
4. Cotton balls.
5. Powder puff.
6. Sponge.
7. Baby oil or Ponds cold cream.

Step 1 Cover your whole face with a very thin layer of white greasepaint or pan make-up. This layer will be thin enough for your natural face to show through. Remove the streaks if any.

Step 2 Apply your black greasepaint to make out your facial features. A good black eyebrow pencil would also do the job. Don't make your mouth or your eyes larger than they are. This black can be applied with the fingers or by using a brush.

Step 3 Apply the talcum powder to your face with the powder puff. Your whole face needs to feel quite dry.

Step 4 Use your cotton balls to brush off any excess powder.

Step 5 Wet sponge lightly and dab over the face. This will help your make-up to set.

The make-up can be easily removed with baby oil or cold cream. As I mentioned before, some make-ups can be removed with soap and water.

Usually when miming (unless dressed as a clown), I have used black leotards and black tights or slacks.

The Loud Silence

This mime is an Advent one. I would suggest that it could be used for Senior Secondary, youth groups and parishes.

The mime itself is short and simple and has been based on the passage of scripture from Matthew 25:35-46.

You will need one person to be the central figure of the mime as well as four groups of people, perhaps three or four people in each group.

Each of the groups will be in ordinary clothes. One group can be dressed as children with lots of toys. A second group can be a family with boxes and boxes of gift-wrapped Christmas presents. A third group could be a group of women dressed in very good clothes and the last group can be a group of partymakers with hats, balloons and whistles. They will also need a large, sign that reads CHRISTMAS. This sign will later be hung around the mimist's head.

I see the main mimist dressed as a clown, but this is entirely up to you.

The mimist enters the sanctuary and looks around. From the expression on his face, the congregation can see that he is not very happy. From his movements we learn that he is hungry and lonely. He sits down upon the steps of the sanctuary (if there are any) and huddles into a tiny ball.

The first group of people enter the scene. From their clothes we can see that they are a group of children carrying many toys. They are laughing and having fun. They come to a still position and freeze. The mimist looks up startled and looks at them. He then faces the congregation with a puzzled look on his face. He once again looks at the children. He walks very, very carefully over to the group and peers at them. He then walks around the group, occasionally looking at the congregation.

The group unfreezes and begins to play with their toys, still laughing. The mimist tries to join in the group to play, but each time he is pushed away. He tries several times and each time is rebuffed by the group. At last he gives up and goes back to his original position on the step. The group of children skip off, still laughing, and as they pass the mimist, they turn their heads obviously the other way.

A few seconds pass and the second group enters. This is the family group. They have been Christmas shopping with the children. Each member of the family is laden down with many presents gift-wrapped in brightly coloured paper. Perhaps even, one member may have a Christmas tree under one arm. They stop and stand in a group and start to sing carols.

The mimist upon hearing their voices raises his head and looks in their direction. He stands and once again very, very slowly goes over to the group and walks around them. Once again, he occasionally looks at the congregation.

The mimist then bends down on one knee and begs for some food or money from the group. They look at him, turn their heads the other way and continue to sing their Christmas carols. The mimist gets up and tries from another direction to gain their attention. Once again the family look at him and turn away. At last the leader of the group suggests that they move on and so they do. The mimist is left alone. And once again he goes back to his original position.

A few seconds pass and the third group enters. This is the group of partymakers. It is obvious that they are going to a party. They have many different coloured balloons, party hats on their heads, streamers draped around their bodies and whistles in their mouths. They stop and freeze. Once again the mimist goes over to the group very, very slowly. He stops and looks at them and as before, he circles the group, occasionally looking at the congregation. Once again, he tries to convey to the group that he is lonely and hungry but they too like the last group turn their heads and face the other way. The mimist tries several times but each time he is ignored by the party-makers. At last he gives up and goes back to his sitting position.

After a few seconds the partymakers suddenly see him. Laughing and making rather a large noise, they run over to where the mimist is sitting. They skip around him in a circle and make fun of him. At last one of the partymakers hangs a large sign on the mimist which reads CHRISTMAS. They then skip around him a few more times making fun of him and then they run off.

The mimist is very upset. He looks at the congregation. He then very slowly looks at the sign hanging around his neck. He points out each letter carefully. He then looks at the congregation as if to say, 'What is CHRIST-MAS?' He then stands and takes the sign off from around his neck and walks over to where one of the toys from the first group has been left, and puts the sign on the floor near the toy. 'Is this Christmas?', he asks the congregation.

He then moves over to where one small Christmas present has been left lying on the floor. Once again, he places the sign near it and asks the congregation the same question. He finally goes over to where some streamers from the party group has been left and he picks them up. He asks the congregation the same question again. He shakes his head and walks around the sanctuary looking lost.

He then looks up to notice the cross hanging in the church. He goes up to it and places the sign which reads CHRISTMAS at the foot of the cross or in view of the congregation. He then slowly walks off the sanctuary.

At the conclusion of the mime, a person from the congregation comes up to the sanctuary and reads the passage of scripture from Matthew 24:35-40 and 42-46.

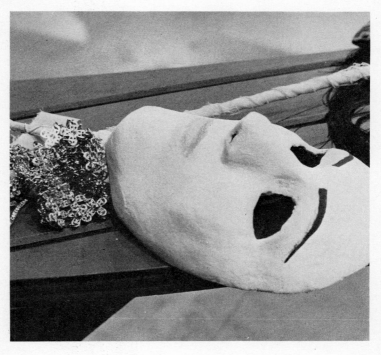

Dances for you to try

Mary's Song

(From *The Christmas Book*, Moira Eastman & Wendy Poussard. Dove Communications.)
This dance will be done in a circle. Children start by holding hands.

1.	
I'm happy, I'm happy.	Two steps and hop starting on the right foot and travelling around to the right.
My heart sings and dances.	Four walking steps around to the right. Last walk, all face the centre of the circle.
God fills us with his grace.	Step into the circle on the right foot and point the left toe behind. Raise arms high.
He makes our home his dwelling place.	Step back on the left foot and bring the right foot in to join the left. Let go of your partner's hands and bring your arms down to waist height. Palms facing up.
I say yes to my God. His good news is my answer.	Swing arms up into the 'V' position.

Chorus	
God promised he would care for us. He will always be there for us.	Taking hands and holding them high, walk around in the circle for sixteen counts. Last count, all face the centre of the circle.
His promises come true.	Children cross their arms in front of their chests and then swing them up into the 'V' position.
There is nothing our God cannot do.	Step to the right and point your left toe to the side. Hold, and repeat to the other side.

2.	
God came to a poor girl, Mary of Galilee.	Bring your arms slowly down to your side.
He chose her for his own, and in her his power was shown.	With arms still at side, walk around in your own circle to the right for four walks.
I am not proud or famous. But God does his work through me.	Facing the centre of the circle, raise arms up into the 'V' position.

Chorus	
3.	
I'm happy, I'm happy.	Two steps and hop to the right, starting on the right foot and travelling to the right.
I sing my song of praise.	Four walking steps around in the circle, travelling to the right. Last walk, all face the centre of the circle.
God puts down mighty kings.	Kneel on the left knee and bend slightly over the right knee.
Fills the hungry with good things.	Stand and bring the arms into the 'V' position.
He watches over us and is with us all our days.	With arms still raised, take four walks in your own circle going to the right.

Chorus

God fills us with his grace.

He makes our home his dwelling place.

There is nothing our God cannot do.

God puts down mighty kings.

The Spirit is Coming

(From *The Pentecost Book*, Moira Eastman, Dove Communications.)
This dance is also done in a circle.

Something's happening, listen and see.	Raise arms slowly to the 'V' position.
The Spirit is coming to you and me.	Using the 'Spirit' gesture, bring your hands down to the centre of your chest.
'Go to Jerusalem', Jesus said.	Step to the right and point the left toe. Move arms to the right to suggest 'going forth'.
Don't be downhearted; you'll find a friend.	Both feet together and bring arms to the side; lower head slightly.
My Spirit will come upon you as you wait and pray.	Repeat 'Spirit' gesture.
His love will strengthen you day by day.	Arms raised to the 'V' position.
His friends and his mother together stay. They chose Matthias to fill Judas's place.	Take one step into the circle and place hands on each other's shoulders.
Then the Spirit comes like the wind above.	Turning to the right, each person spins off back to their own place; two turns.
To fill their hearts with the fire of love.	Facing the centre of the circle, bring hands into your heart and stretch them into the 'V' position.

Peter's not afraid now.

Come and belong.

arts that open to love open to all.	Repeat the previous gesture, but kneel. Instead of taking your hands to the 'V' position, extend them to the side.
er's not afraid now, stands ight and tall.	Stand still with arms to the side.
uts to the crowd, 'Come and ong.	Hands cupped to your mouth.
r in the Spirit we are made ong'.	'Spirit' gesture and raising arms quickly to the 'V' position.
ung people see a world that is w.	Still facing the centre of the circle, walk four steps into your own circle taking your hands to your eyes and then up to the 'V' position.
d people dream now their dream rue.	Kneel on the left knee and bow over the right knee. Hands into the chest. Straighten body and raise arms high and then open them to the side, shoulder height.
aling and holiness the church has eived.	Stand with hands still outstretched.
e Spirit lives on in those who lieve.	The 'Spirit' gesture and finally raising arms to the 'V' position.

For the Spirit makes us strong.

Old people dream now.

Their dream is true.

Creative movement in the classroom

In the chapter on movement prayers, we had a look at how you and your class can begin choreographing simple prayer movements. In this chapter we will take a look at how you can use creative movement to help your class achieve a deeper understanding and love of the Bible.

The aim of the following ideas is to produce various feelings within the children and to give them a concrete experience from which discussion between teacher and pupil can develop.

It is important to remember not to rush through each of the lessons but to take time so that the children can fully enter into the experience you are trying to create.

The Father's love

Stage 1

Close your eyes and think about someone you love very much . . . a friend perhaps . . . your family . . . a brother or sister . . . one of your parents . . . Make a mental picture of this person.

If you could give them one present only, what would you give them? What would be the greatest thing that you could do for that person?

Take the gift you have chosen and describe it using your hands only. What is the size of the gift? How is the gift used?

Out of love for us, God has given us many special gifts . . . He has given us the gift of *ourselves* . . . the gift of *life* . . .

(The next few exercises are to make the children more aware of their bodies and how they can use them.)

Scripture (Genesis 1:27)

> 'God created man in the image of himself,
> in the image of God he created him,
> male and female, he created them.'

God is all perfect, all loving and all beautiful. He made us like him. We are beautiful people and can be all loving too.

How many ways can you move your head . . . You may grip it or nod it . . . Try shaking it . . . now rolling it . . . How else can you move it?

How many different movements can you do with your neck? . . . Try twisting it . . . now craning it . . . now pulling it in . . .

Now try wrinkling your nose . . . raising your eyebrows . . . changing the shape of your mouth . . . fluttering your eyelids . . .

Our hands can do many things . . . clap sharply . . . stretch your fingers . . . now clench your fists . . . now spread your fingers apart . . .

Shrug your shoulders up and down . . . wriggle them . . . droop them . . .

Swing your arms loosely in all different directions . . .

Now do the same with your legs . . . first the right . . . then the left . . .

Our arms, legs, head, yes, our whole body was created by God. Out of love for us he gave us the gift of life.

Let us use our whole body to thank him for this special gift.

Let's create for him our own bodily prayer . . .

I	Put both feet together and bring your hands into your chest.
Praise you, Father	Raise both arms up into a 'V' position.
For the gift	Cup both hands as if you were receiving a special gift.
Of life.	Spin around twice on your own spot with your arms stretched out to your sides.
Prayer:	Heavenly Father, you created me. You breathed into me your Holy Spirit. The heart you gave me, you held first in your own hands. I thank you that I am wonderfully made.

Suitable songs that could be used to supplement this lesson are 'Say To The Lord, I Love You' which is from the *Kids Praise 2* album from Maranatha and 'Thank You, God' from Carey Landry.

Stage 2

Remember that special gift that you chose for your loved one? Well, God your Father has given you other special gifts as well as the gift of life.

Recall in your mind some of the things that you can do . . . you may be a good artist or you may be good at sport. Sometimes it takes us a while to find the things that we are good at. These special gifts from our Father are called *talents*.

Let's take time to thank God for your talents . . .

Find a space of your own . . . plant your feet firmly on the floor . . . just a little apart. Close your eyes . . . don't move your feet but stretch your arms as far as you can in every direction. Explore the space around you. Breathe slowly and deeply . . . now, open your eyes . . . It is in this space that you are going to move.

What is that special talent that God has given you?

(Teachers note, some people may need some help and encouragement to recognise their special talents.)

In your own space, mime out your special talent.

Scripture (Matthew 25:14-30)

Out of love for us, God gave us the special gift of our talents. By using them, we are saying to God our Father: 'Thank you'.

Let's use our whole body to say 'thanks'.

Close your eyes and think of your special talents. Cup your hands in front of your chest and try to imagine that you are holding your special gift from God in your hands . . . now in your heart and mind stretch your arms up into the 'V' position as you say 'thanks'.

To say an even bigger 'thanks', you may like to kneel on one knee, and as you say 'thanks', raise your whole body to a standing position with your arms in the 'V' position.

Perhaps you can think of some other way that you can say 'thanks' to God our Father using your body.

It is important to remember that whatever bodily gesture we use, our 'thanks' must come from deep within our hearts.

Once again suitable songs that could be used at this point are 'Make a Joyful Noise' and 'Praise God' which can both be found on *Kids Praise 2* by Maranatha.

Stage 3

The greatest gift that God our Father has given us is the gift of his only Son Jesus.

Scripture (John 3:16)

> 'Yes, God so loved the world
> that he gave his only Son,
> so that everyone who believes in him
> may not be lost
> but have eternal life.'

God reveals his great love for each one of us through his Son Jesus and the cross. Jesus also showed his love for us.

Scripture (John 15:13)

> 'A man can have no greater love than to lay down his life for his friends.'

Jesus died so that we may be freed from sin.

Try to imagine that you are carrying a heavy load on your back . . . perhaps a load of bricks . . . each time you take a few steps, feel the load getting heavier and heavier all the time . . . walk around in your own space . . . Can you feel your load getting heavy . . . what are your steps like . . . are they short and brisk or long and heavy?

Now relax . . .

This time, imagine that you are in a desert . . . the sun is blazing and the heat intense . . . you have been walking for a long time . . . perhaps you are lost . . . show by your steps and your body how you are feeling . . . don't forget your facial expressions . . . is your throat dry . . . feel the dirt and dust around your feet . . . perhaps you may even stumble and fall once or twice.

Scripture (Luke 22:33-38, 44-46)

Now imagine that you are Jesus . . . the cross that you are going to carry has been placed across your shoulders . . . by your body posture, show how you are going to carry your cross . . . feel the dryness in your mouth . . . the perspiration trickling down your back . . . the dust gathering around your feet . . . feel the stares of the people as you pass by . . . feel the weight of the cross increase . . . you fall.

Here the music that I would suggest would be the prelude to 'The Lord's Supper' by John Michael Talbot.

The Eucharistic Acclamations remind us that Christ died, that he rose and that he will come again in glory. This is all part of God's plan for us.

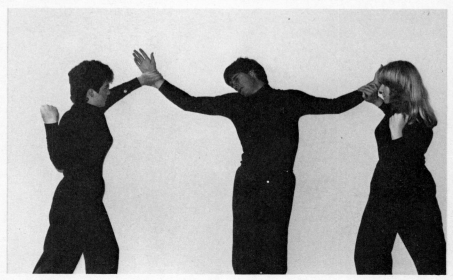

Acclamation

Christ has died,	Make a cross with your hands in front of your chest and kneel on your left knee.
Christ is risen,	Still kneeling, swing your arms in a circular motion outwards to stretch to the sides.
Christ will come again.	Stand and take your arms up into the 'V' position.

The dances I have chosen to accompany this section are 'Jesus' from the *Kids Praise* Album by Maranatha and 'Jesus we Know You' from Joe Wise (Dove Communications).

Final Prayer

Heavenly Father,	Arms swing up into a 'V' position.
your love for us is so great.	Swing arms around to cross in front of your body and to end back in the 'V' position.
We cannot measure its height or depth.	Stretch up high and then crouch down low.
You show us your love by giving us	Stand on your two feet and cup your hands in front of you.
the gift of life,	Swirl around once on your own spot.
the gift of our talents,	Arms spread out to side.
the gift of Jesus.	Make a cross with your hands in front of your chest.
For all these gifts,	Cup your hands in front of your body.
we thank you.	Swing arms up quickly into the 'V' position.

You are the potter, we are the clay

For this theme, you will need your Bible, some plasticine, some examples of pottery and the record 'Abba Father' by Carey Landry.

Begin by giving each child a piece of the plasticine and ask them to mould it into as many different shapes as possible. This exercise should take no longer than about five minutes.

How many different shapes could you make . . . was the plasticine easy or hard to mould . . . how did the plasticine feel in your hands?

Now stand and find a space of your own to move in . . . now try to imagine that you are lying in your own space, feeling very heavy . . . you feel lifeless . . . all life has drained out of your body . . . you feel very limp. Now try to imagine that you are being moulded and shaped . . . your body is being pushed and pulled in all directions . . . feel yourself twisting and turning . . . now freeze. What shape have you been moulded into?

Now reverse the role . . . imagine that you are the potter and you are working with a large piece of clay . . . you are going to make a life-size statue . . . show me by using your body how you are rolling and shaping the very large piece of clay. Step back and admire your work.

Scripture (Jeremiah 18:1-6)

After reading the scripture passage, discuss it with your children. Ask them what a potter does and how a piece of pottery is made. Mention all the different pieces of equipment that he may use, e.g. the wheel. Look at and discuss the examples of pottery that you have. Talk about the time and care that the potter takes with each piece. Look at the pieces of pottery and you will see that no two pieces are exactly the same. It is very hard to match pottery pieces exactly.

How is God like the potter?

How are we continually being moulded and shaped?

Invite a potter to visit your class and talk about his craft or visit a potter's shop.

The song I have chosen to finish this theme is 'Abba Father' from Carey Landry. This song is very good for the children to improvise movement. Perhaps they could feel that they are being moulded and shaped by the potter, God. Encourage the children to explore their movements and at the same time feel that they are being moulded into the type of person that God wants them to be.

Creation

For this theme you will need your Bible and the record 'Peer Gynt'. The track used in this theme is the 'Morning Suite'. You will also need a tambourine.

Spread yourselves out on the floor and find your own space to move in. Once you have found your spot, lie down in it and completely relax. Let your breath come and go easily . . . feel all the movement completely drain away from you . . . close your eyes loosely . . . listen to the sound of your own heartbeat . . . imagine that you are a tiny seed planted in the soil . . . feel the soil all around you . . . is it hard . . . does it feel warm . . . do you feel snug with the soil all wrapped around you? Curl up as small as possible in your own hole . . .

When you hear the sound of the tambourine, imagine that you are now starting to grow slowly . . . (*shake tambourine*) start spreading your roots out slowly into the soil . . . pushing your way through the tight earth . . . slowly . . . very slowly . . . begin to move both arms out to the sides . . . pushing . . . pushing through the soil . . . keep moving until all your roots have spread out into the soil. Start to shoot upwards . . . towards the light . . . splitting the soil in two as you reach for the sunlight . . .

We are now going to work together in pairs . . . the important thing to remember is that you are not going to move as two separate seeds, but as *one* seed . . . find your starting position and begin very, very slowly . . . moving together as one seed . . .

(Repeat this exercise again and again, increasing the number in each group.)

Scripture (Genesis 2:4-7)

Find your own space on the floor again . . . this time, lie flat on your back and once again feel completely relaxed . . . be aware of your breathing again . . . stay with this awareness for a while . . . as the music begins, I would like you to imagine that you are Adam and that for the very first time in your life you are feeling what it is like to be able to move . . . Slowly, very slowly begin to move . . . perhaps first your head . . . move it around and around . . . then your eyes . . . open them . . . blink . . . now your hands . . . move each finger very very slowly . . . be aware of the movements as you make them . . . now your whole arm . . . move it slowly out to the side . . . once again being aware of each movement as you make it . . . Next try the legs . . . moving them slowly in all directions as you go . . . move your toes . . . wriggle them . . . bend your knees . . . after exploring all the different ways in which you can move your body on the floor . . . slowly, very slowly begin to stand . . . stretch . . . stretch . . . even more in all the different directions . . . stretch upwards . . . stretch to the sides . . . bend at the waist forwards and backwards . . . stretching as far as you can in all directions.

How do you think that Adam would have felt, coming to life and seeing the world for the first time?

The Ten Lepers

For this theme, you will need a tambourine and your Bible.

As with the last theme, ask the children to relax on the floor. Discuss with them ways in which they can move their body. They can bend it . . . twist it . . . shake it . . . roll it on the floor . . .

Ask the children to give you examples of these.

While relaxing on the floor, think of as many ways as you can to move around on the floor . . . at the sound of the tambourine begin . . . when you hear the sound again, change your movement to another, and so on . . .

Give the children a few minutes to explore as many movements as they can. Repeat this exercise, standing.

When you hear the tambourine, I would like you to show me a twisted shape . . . (*shake tambourine*) . . . now show me a straight shape (*shake tambourine again*) . . . Repeat this a few times, getting the children to follow each twisted shape with a straight shape.

Call the children together and ask them what they know about leprosy. Why were lepers outcasted in Jesus' time? What did people do to warn others that lepers were coming? Where does leprosy strike you?

Ask the children to decide where leprosy has struck them . . . In what part of their body . . . is it an arm . . . or a leg . . . perhaps in the back?

To the beat of the tambourine, move around like a leper, keeping in mind where leprosy has struck you. When you hear the tambourine shake, recoil into a tight group, hiding behind each other . . .

Scripture (Luke 17:11-19)

Emmaus . . . a Gospel Play and Dance

This short play and dance movement would be suitable for Senior Primary o
Junior Secondary children.

You will also need the song 'Are not our hearts' from *Hi God*! by Care
Landry.

Players:	Narrator
	Jesus
	Two disciples
Narrator:	Two of the disciples were on their way to a village called Emmaus, whic was seven miles from Jerusalem, and they were talking together about all tha had happened. Now as they talked this over, Jesus himself came up an walked by their side; but something prevented them from recognising him.
Jesus:	What matters are you discussing as you walk along?
Narrator:	They stopped short, their faces downcast.
All:	'Are not our hearts' (Sing one verse only.)
Narrator:	Then one of them answered him.
Disciple 1:	You must be the only person in Jerusalem who does not know the things tha have been happening here over the last few days.
Jesus:	What things?
Disciple 2:	All about Jesus of Nazareth who proved that he was a great prophet by th things that he said and did in the sight of God and the whole people; and ho our chief priests and leaders handed him over to be sentenced to death an crucified.
Disciple 1:	Two whole days have passed since it happened; and some women from ou group have astounded us: they went along to the tomb in the early morning and when they did not find the body, they came back to tell us that they ha seen a vision of an angel who declared that Jesus was alive.
All:	'Are not our hearts' (Sing one verse only.)

Disciple 2:	Some of our people went to the tomb and found everything exactly as the women had reported, but of him they saw nothing.
Disciple 1:	It is nearly evening and the day is over.
Narrator:	So they invited the stranger in to stay with them.
All:	'Are not our hearts' (Sing one verse only.)
Narrator:	And it was while he was with them at the table that he took the bread and blessed it, he broke it and handed it to them. And immediately their eyes were open and they recognised him, but he had vanished from their sight. Then they said to each other.
Disciple 2:	Did not our hearts burn within us as he talked with us on the road and explained the scriptures to us?
All:	'Are not our hearts' (Sing all verses.)
Movement:	This dance can be done in a circle by any number of children.
Verse 1:	Facing anti-clockwise, the children walk around in the circle starting on the right foot. At the same time they bring their hands into the centre of their chests and bring them up into the 'V' position. This is done four times.
Verse 2:	Facing the centre of the circle, the children take hands and walk four steps into the centre of the circle at the same time raising hands up high. They then take four walks backwards and bring arms down low. This is repeated.
Verse 3:	The children kneel facing the centre of the circle. All kneel on their left knee. The body is slightly bent over the right knee. Arms are at sides and slowly raised high into the 'V' position. Then the arms are waved from right to left and repeated. The arms are brought down to the sides and the whole action is repeated.

This is the complete movement. As the song is sung in a round, it would be appropriate to have two circles. The whole group would start the movement together and as the song broke into the round, so would the two circles so that it was danced as a round.

An Advent Play with Movement

A movement/drama for Upper Primary and Junior Secondary taken from the Gospel of St Luke.

Scene One

Narrator: This is the Gospel according to Luke.

The angel Gabriel was sent by God as a messenger into a small town in Galilee which was called Nazareth.

In this town the angel would find a young girl who was engaged to a man called Joseph. Her name was Mary. The angel found Mary in her home and spoke to her.

Gabriel: Rejoice, Mary! The Lord is with you.

Mary: What do you mean?

Gabriel: Mary, do not be frightened. God is happy with you. You have been chosen from all other women to bear a son, and you must name him Jesus. He will be great and will be called the Son of the Most High. He will receive the throne of his ancestor David.

Mary: How can this happen? I don't understand.

Gabriel: God's Holy Spirit will come upon you. Your child will be holy and will be called the Son of God. Nothing is impossible to God.

Mary: Let all that you have said happen.

Scene Two

Narrator: Mary set out on a long journey to visit her cousin Elizabeth who was also expecting a baby. On reaching Elizabeth's house, Mary went in.

Elizabeth: Of all the women, Mary, you are the most blessed, and blessed also the baby within your womb. Why am I honoured by a visit from the mother of my Lord? Mary, you are blessed because you believed the promise made to you by God would be fulfilled.

(Here I would suggest two ideas. Firstly, the Magnificat could be spoken as well as dramatised through bodily movement by Mary or spoken by the narrator while Mary interprets it through movement.)

Magnificat	**Movements**
[M]y soul proclaims the greatness of [the] Lord and my Spirit exults in God [my] Saviour;	Facing people with feet together, bring both arms up into a 'V' position and then slowly step backwards on the right foot bring arms down to the side. Bend over the front foot which should be pointed.
[Bec]ause he has looked upon his [low]ly handmaid.	Stand back up into original position with arms back into the 'V' position.
[Ye]s, from this day forward all [gen]erations shall call me blessed,	Take both arms to the left side with the right hand on top of the left and bring both arms slowly forward across the body to extend to the right side.
[For] the Almighty has done great [thin]gs for me and Holy is his name,	Bring both arms up overhead with hands together and palms facing outwards as if framing God's name with your hands.
[And] his mercy reaches from age to [age] for those who fear him.	Bring arms down to extend outwards with palms facing upwards. Then take right arm to the right side and left arm to the left side.
[He] has shown the power of his arm,	Raise right arm into the air with fist closed and bring left arm down to side.
[He] has routed the proud of heart.	Kneel on left knee and bring both hands into the centre of your chest. Bow head slightly.
[He] has pulled down princes from [the]ir thrones	Stay in the above position.
[And] exalted the lowly.	Raise head and stand with both feet together and arms in the 'V' position.
[Th]e hungry he has filled with good [thin]gs,	Step to the right side on the right foot and lunge to the right pointing the left toe. As you do this bring both hands into your mouth as if 'begging'.
[The] rich sent empty away.	Stepping back on to both feet, take left arm out to side with palm facing erect. Head turned to the right.
[He] has come to the help of Israel his [ser]vant, mindful of his mercy —	Step forward and bring both arms extended forward with palms facing upwards.
[Acc]ording to the promise he made to [our] ancestors —	Step backwards keeping hands in the same position.
[H]is mercy to Abraham and to his [des]cendants for ever.	Kneel on both knees with arms in the 'V' position. Sit back slightly on knees.

53

Dancing Christmas Carols

The times during the Church's year when I really enjoy choreographing dances is during Advent/Christmas and Lent/Easter. I enjoy working with Christmas carols in particular as the tunes are lively and lend themselves to a wide variety of dance steps. Through the dance, you can create an atmosphere of joy for all those watching so that they too may want to 'join in the dance'. Christmas carols are a great way to begin dancing in your school, youth group or parish. The dances are so choreographed that anyone can join in the dance without actually being a dancer. They are also created for people of all ages.

The first carol I have chosen is an old English carol which dates back to the 18th century and is well known by all.

God rest ye merry, gentlemen

God rest ye merry, gentlemen, let nothing you dismay, for Jesus Christ our Saviour was born on Christmas day,	Make one large circle and, facing inwards, hold hands. Then, take one step to the right and bending left foot in behind right and take another step to the right on the right foot and bring left foot in to meet right. Repeat this step to the left, right and then left again.
To save us all from Satan's power when we had gone astray.	Take four running steps into the centre of the circle commencing on the right foot and at the same time bend over slightly from the waist with arms forward into centre of the circle. At this stage you are still holding hands. Then take four running steps backwards out of the circle starting on the right foot bringing hands up into the air and body straight.
Chorus	
O tidings of comfort and joy, comfort and joy!	Holding hands up high, walk around in the circle going to the right and commencing with the right foot (seven steps).

These steps make up the whole dance. It is interesting to note that centuries ago, carols were sung and danced in a type of stanza-chorus form. When the stanza came round, the group would stand still and sing. Sometimes the leader would stand in the middle of the circle. When they came to the chorus, the group would dance around in the circle as they sang.

Angels we have heard on high

This is one of my favourites and is a traditional French carol. Once again, this dance is done in a circle with twelve people.

gels we have heard on high, etly singing o'er the plains,	Facing the centre of the circle and holding hands, the group proceeds to the right doing the Greek Vine step commencing on the right foot.
the mountains in reply oing still their joyous strains.	Repeat to the left.
orus	
. . . ri-a	Mark each person in your circle 1, 2, 3 and 4. 　During the chorus for the first *Gloria*, person number 1 runs into the centre of the circle followed by person 2, 3 and lastly 4.
xcelsis Deo.	Take four steps backwards to original place bringing arms down in front of you and finally bringing them to your sides.
eat the chorus again.	
pherds, why this jubilee? y your joyous strains prolong?	Taking hands in the circle once more, raise them up high and walk around in the circle going to the right and commencing on the right foot (eight steps).
, what may the tidings be, ch inspire your heavenly song.	Repeat to the left.
orus	Repeat chorus movement.
ne to Bethlehem and see a whose birth the angels sing:	Forming a right hand star (i.e. facing the right of your circle with the left hand pointed into the centre of the circle) walk around to the right and bring the left arm out to the people 'inviting' them to 'come and see' (eight steps).
ne, adore on bended knee ist the Lord, the new-born g.	Repeat the above movement to the left.
orus	Repeat chorus movement.

　The reason that I have choreographed these carols as folk dances is that carols are from a folk tradition and therefore need to be danced as folk dances. The early carols would have been done this way also.

Dance in the Bible

In the Old Testament, we find that dance is mentioned quite a few times. It appears to have been a special feature of Israelite worship. The Israelites used a variety of instruments to accompany their dancing: hand drums made from animal skins, pipes, lutes, lyres, harps and cymbal as well as hand bells. Most of the dances were done in circles and the choreography was limited. Their dances were often quite vigorous.

Our first reference to dance is in Exodus 15:20-21 where the prophetess Miriam took her timbrel and danced a dance of thanksgiving after crossing the Red Sea.

'Sing of Yahweh: he has covered himself in glory,
horse and rider he has thrown into the sea.'

Many of the Psalms invite us to praise God through dance and movement.

Psalm 30:11
'You have turned my mourning into dancing.'

Psalm 47:1
'Clap your hands, all you people acclaim God with shouts of joy.'

Psalm 87:9
'And there will be princes dancing there.'

Psalm 134:2
'Stretch out your hands before the sanctuary, bless Yahweh night after night.'

Psalm 150:4
'Praise him with drums and dancing.'

Other references can be found in 2 Samuel 6:4 where we find David dancing with all his might before the ark of the Covenant. Other references can be found in Judges 11:34, Ecclesiastes 3:4, Lament 5:15, Jeremiah 31:1 and Zephaniah 3:17.

In the New Testament, there are not many direct references to dance but in Romans 12:1 and 1 Corinthians 6:19 we are reminded that we should use our body to glorify God. Other New Testament references are Matthew 11:16 Luke 6:22-23 and Luke 15:25. In the New Testament, there seems to be none of the dancing and music making that was a special feature of the Israelite worship. Reasons for this vary but one seems to be the fact that the Christians met inside houses where there would have been hardly any room for the dance to take place.

After the New Testament, there seems to be little or no evidence of dance or drama until the 4th century where we know that it took place in some churches. St Augustine spoke out against dance because of its association with pagan festivals. He encouraged the people and the church to understand the literal call to 'dance' in a more symbolic way as well as in a more 'spiritual' way. Augustine was quoting from Psalm 149 and 150 when he said,

'Let them praise his name in chorus.
What do we mean by "chorus"?
A "chorus" is a unison of singers.
When we sing in "chorus",
let us sing in concord.'

However, the word 'chorus' comes from a Latin word *chorea* which is a translation from a Hewbrew word meaning 'to dance in a circle'. Certainly Augustine's interpretation shifted the meaning.

It was later during the reign of Pope Gregory the Great that dance was officially excluded from the Catholic liturgy. Mime and drama were also to disappear along with the dance.

Other words that we use today where the meaning of the word has been changed are:

rejoice;   in Aramaic (the language Jesus spoke) this word meant to leap or to dance. When Jesus told the people to rejoice, they would have taken this to be an invitation to dance. He certainly would have danced too as he was a Jew and dancing was a very important part of Jewish worship;

carol: from the Italian word *carolare* meaning a medieval ring dance accompanied by music and song.

Today, there is a renewed interest in dance and drama in the church. Many groups are emerging within the Australian churches.

He will exult with joy over you,
he will renew you by his love;
he will dance with shouts of joy for you
as on a day of festival. (*Zephaniah 3:17*)

What to wear

I could not begin to count the number of people who have asked me 'What d
you wear?'.

It depends on the type of music you are dancing to. If you are dancing to
rather light and bouncy tune, then a gown made from a heavy material suc
as a velvet would not be suitable. It also depends on the season of the yea
Sometimes inexperienced dancers such as children may find it difficult
move in a long gown. I tend to stay away from white gowns. In our danc
group, we use celebration colours: golds, blues, greens, reds. We also kee
in mind the season of the Church year, e.g. during Advent and Lent, we wea
mauve.

Try to avoid gowns that cling to the body. These can be a source of
distraction to those watching. Loose fitting garments are also easier to mov
in. If you are using one set of gowns for your school or parish, then loos
fitting ones are far more practicable as one size fits all.

For the boys or men, I suggest long trousers with a coloured tunic, shirt of
T-shirt.

When dancing, we usually go bare foot. This can cause some problems
your church is old or the floor is cold. 'Moses, take off your shoes for th
place on which you stand is holy ground' (*Exodus 3:6*).

Remember when choosing your material for your gowns, try to choose on
that is washable, does not crease easily and will not show too much dirt.

Arm Movements